Spells for
CATS

Spells for
CATS

Daisy Pepper

Illustrations by Lauren Dorman

Kyle Cathie Limited

This book is dedicated to my favourite sleeping companions: Clarence, Pharaoh, Cleopatra, Bella, Iddy Diddy, Greta and Buster. Thank you all for allowing me a corner of my duvet.

I'm also grateful to my mother for tempering my feline idolatry with realism and my husband (another favourite sleeping companion) for holding our kids while I wrote this book.

Cheers to everyone who shared their cat stories and to KC and CT for believing in this project despite being dog people at heart.

First published in Great Britain in 2001 by
Kyle Cathie Limited
122 Arlington Road
London NW1 7HP
general.enquiries@kyle-cathie.com
www.kylecathie.com

ISBN 1 85626 427 0

Edited by Caroline Taggart
Designed by Button Design Co
Production by Lorraine Baird and Sha Huxtable
Photographs on pages 28 and 70 by Juliet Piddington

Daisy Pepper is hereby identified as the author of this work in accordance with Section 77 of the Copyright, Designs and Patents Act 1988.

A Cataloguing in Publication record for this title is available from the British Library.

Printed in Singapore by Tien-Wah Press

Contents

Introduction 6

Good cat practice 9

Catnip communion candle 12

Blanket magic 14

Charging the blanket 16

Communing spell 18

Egyptian temple rattle 20

Moon pompom 22

Lucky cat amulet 24

Crossed legs spell 26

Fleas away 28

Shooo flies 30

Old cat retirement patch 32

An udjat eye for protection . . . 34

Cat flu spell 36

Pill popper 38

Tom's poultice 40

Hot cat summer soother 42

Traffic talisman 44

Curiosity… 46

Nine lives top-up 48

Wild bird spell 50

Diana's hunting spell 52

Impossibly forgiving 54

To banish foul bane 56

Righteous habit, wrong place . . 58

High-rise spell 60

Travel cat 62

Cerridwen's shape-shifting spell . 64

Scaredy cat 66

Lie down dog 68

Cat/dog love potion 70

Bully bane hex 72

Stray cat divination 74

Funeral reading 76

Herb garden memorial 78

Attracting the right cat mate . . 80

Space cleansing 82

Naming ceremony 84

New cat on the block 86

Six sabbats for cats 88

    Samhain 89

    Winter solstice 89

    Imbolg 90

    Beltane 90

    Summer solstice 91

    Lughnasa 91

Glossary 92

Introduction

More than 4000 years ago, cats realised there were certain advantages to living with humans. Revered by the Egyptians as gods on earth, it is little wonder that they came in from the wild and allowed themselves to be seen as "domesticated".

This was and is, of course, an illusion. Cats will never become domesticated in the dog or goldfish sense of the word. Cats merely tolerate humans in the pursuit of the good life. Having established themselves as objects of worship they quickly moved in on the courtiers – the laps of pharaohs and their wives were soon their favoured domain.

Unlike modern humans, who have a tendency to try to curb a cat's instincts, the clever Egyptians allowed cats to express themselves freely. This included joint hunting expeditions where cats and humans worked together to bag a crane or catch some fish. Nowadays there's much nostalgia among cats for this golden age. What they miss most is not the willing worshipper, feather pillows or food on tap – these things are still their prerogative. No, what they hanker after is the use of magic in their everyday lives.

The Egyptians used more spells and rituals than any other culture before or since. But it is impossible to tell whether it was the cats who taught the humans or the other way round. Maybe it took both.

Whichever it was, one thing is certain: cats are extremely knowledgeable and responsive to spells from all pagan cultures. Indeed, it was a white-spotted cat who sparked the first English witchcraft trial in Essex in 1565. One woman was hanged and another imprisoned having apparently received magical tuition from the cat. I don't doubt they did, but I'm sure it wasn't the cat's idea to use the magic for evil ends. It's just not their style. He probably wished he'd kept his heritage to himself.

So, how to persuade cats to share their knowledge once more? The spells in this book should whet their appetite. Once you've gathered the ingredients and begun to weave your magic, cats won't be able to resist. All you need to get started is the kind of problem that may arise when cats and humans live in close proximity. Plus a strong desire to resolve the situation.

Prepare to be amazed.

Good luck and blessed be.

Daisy Pepper

PS You will notice that I never suggest cat ownership, as in "your cat" or "my cat". This is because owning a cat would be like owning the sky: impossible.

PPS You may also note that I refer to cats as "he". This is because "he" has one letter fewer than "she" and is therefore quicker to write. It has absolutely nothing to do with gender preference. Really, I respect all cats, as I do people, as individuals, irrespective of sex — or breed or colour for that matter.

Good cat practice

The following tips are given to help you and cats enjoy many happy spells and years together.

- Cats and candles are a combination requiring close supervision. Tails may be singed or candles knocked over. Beware.

- A sick cat should always be seen by a vet as soon as possible.

- Everyone who lives with a cat should own a cat first-aid book and box. Familiarise yourself with various symptoms and scenarios so that, should anything occur, you can deal calmly with the situation rather than panic.

- Amulets and talismans should be used in conjunction with modern miracles such as vaccinations, regular worming and appropriate use of antibiotics.

🐾 Always look under your car before
driving away from home.

🐾 Always check sheds and garages for cats
if doors have been left open. This is especially
important when you're going away for a few days.

🐾 Unless you are breeding cats and taking ultimate
responsibility for all offspring, do cats a favour and
have them spayed or neutered. It will improve the
quality of life for all cats in the neighbourhood.

🐾 If you are a breeder, ask yourself this: "In pursuit of the
perfect example of a pedigree, do the characteristics
chosen through selective in-breeding hinder or
enhance a cat's mental and physical well-being?"

🐾 Use tidbits sparingly. Cats behave quite like humans where
food is concerned in that they will happily eat whether
hungry or not. Snacking soon becomes a difficult habit to
break. A fat cat is an unhappy and unhealthy cat, however
much he may argue to the contrary.

❧ Cats instinctively hunt. Never punish a cat for bringing home a gift, no matter how inconvenient it is having a live black mamba dropped on the carpet during a dinner party.

❧ Never smack a cat – your karma will be greatly damaged and the cat will never forgive you. Besides, it's pointless. A cat's response to violence is to go and live somewhere else. They may, however, be discouraged from certain activities if you clap loudly when catching them in the act.

❧ Never live with more cats than you and the cats can sensibly accommodate.

❧ Cats prefer gardens to a penthouse dirt-box. If you must introduce a cat to high-rise living, you must argue – successfully – that this life is better than the one you saved him from.

Catnip
communion
candle

Ritual and spell candles should be 100 per cent pure beeswax if possible. Unlike most household candles today, which are made from paraffin, beeswax candles are derived from a totally natural renewable resource. They smell lovely too.

If you wish to add to the scent, rub a few drops of your favourite essential oil on a candle before lighting. Alternatively, put a few drops in the pool of wax around the burning wick.

Better still, imbue undyed beeswax candles with a cat's favourite scent: catnip.

ingredients
large bunch of catnip *(Nepeta cataria)*
100 per cent beeswax undyed candles
shoe box ❧ tissue paper

1. Place candles and catnip in a shoe box with ventilation holes and lined with tissue paper. Store somewhere warm and dark. Turn herbs and candles daily for seven days.

2. Dim the overhead lights, get comfy with the cat, light the candle and commune. Just watch out for singed tails.

Blanket magic

A magical cat needs a magical blanket. So useful to lie on when casting cat spells. Comfy to sleep on, too.

The centre of the blanket depicts a pentacle, the fifth point pointing upwards (like the symbol above). The cat's name is embroidered in the centre.

Each corner of the cloth carries an image representing one of the four elements.

ingredients

A 60cm/2ft square piece of organic, undyed cotton or linen
selection of threads, materials and other collage media,
symbolic of the four elements (air, earth, fire and water)
3m/10ft silver braid or thread (for embroidering
the pentacle and name)
a pencil & a drawing pin & scissors
drawing board or similar surface (even a magazine)

1. To draw the pentacle, fold cloth evenly in half, then in half again to find the centre. Make a mark, then open the cloth and lay out on the board. Stick the drawing pin into the centre.

2. Tie a pencil to a piece of thread attached to the drawing pin. Holding the thread taut, draw a circle. Remove the pin and place it at the top of the circle, midway between two corners of the cloth. Still holding the thread taut, make a mark across the circle's circumference. Put the pin on this mark, repeat and continue around the circle until you end up where you began. Join up alternate marks with straight lines and you will have a five-pointed star within a circle. Embroider this and the cat's name in the centre.

3. Create your emblems of the elements and stitch one in each corner.

4. The cat's blanket is now ready to be magically charged.

Charging the blanket

On a full moon when you and the cat are together, charge the blanket with the energies of the moon. You should work with the lights off and place the blanket near a window where moon beams (the reflected rays of the sun) may shine directly on to it.

ingredients
the blanket (see previous pages)
a full moon & **a crystal**

1. Spread the blanket out in the light of the moonbeams and place the crystal within the star beneath the cat's name.

2. Hold the crystal with your hands on either side of it and put your face up to the moonbeams saying, "The sun via the moon is drawn to the stone, 'tis the force and might of God and Goddess. I implore them now to transform this cloth with a pure and magical essence. May [cat's name] be protected, may [cat's name] be blessed, may [cat's name] always find happiness, harmony and balance."

3. Rub the cat with the blanket, then place the blanket in the cat's bed or on a favourite chair. The magic blanket may help a cat to cope with a visit to the vet, or provide a tranquil haven when your home is chaotic with visitors. Use it as you and your cat see fit.

Communing
spell

To communicate with a cat on his terms, you must search deep
within your subconscious to reawaken your sixth sense. Listen
carefully and you will hear. Think clearly and your thoughts
will be heard. Perform this spell on the night of a full moon.

ingredients
13 dark blue candles & **a piece of blue agate**
a piece of gold, such as a wedding ring
patchouli oil

1. Heat oil in a burner and place candles in a large circle. Sit with the cat, the gold and the agate within the circle. Breathe in through your nose and out through your mouth seven times.

2. Hold the cat, saying, "Come you from the carriage of Freya? Have you flown on Horus' wing? Did Thoth write your name as you basked in the fame of Bastet, purring from her lap? May these deities you love to please now urge you to speak with ease. Speak, cat, speak without fear. Speak and I shall hear."

3. Purring is a good sign. If the cat is wilfully ignoring you, keep trying each full moon.

Egyptian temple rattle

Papier mâché was a favourite medium of the Egyptians, who used it to make everything from scrying bowls to toys. They believed coriander seeds protected the soul.

Use this rattle to lure a cat out of a sulk (for example, following a chastisement for stealing the Sunday roast – again).

ingredients

a small balloon & **tissue paper**
wallpaper paste & **coriander seeds**
gold, blue, black and white paint
varnish & **raffia**

1. Mix torn pieces of tissue paper with the paste and cover the blown-up balloon with them, with a small gap at the bottom. Tie the raffia around the globe like a parcel, leaving an arm's length flowing free. Place more tissue paper over this. When dried, pop the balloon and fill the ball with seeds before closing the gap with more papier mâché.

2. When completely hard, paint it and decorate it with udjat eyes (see page 34), ankh crosses (see page 48) and lotus flowers (illustrated opposite) before varnishing.

3. If a cat is sulking, say,
   "The seeds that served the
      pharaohs sound to your soul.
      Climb down off your sulk
      and come and have a roll."

Moon pompom

For drawing a cat away from work surfaces, favourite plants or the sofa minutes before guests arrive, this spell allows you to play rather than scold. Cats will also enjoy the creative process of unravelling two squidgy balls of wool. When finished, one half of the pompom will glisten while the other remains dark, just as the moon does. It is only from our perspective that the moon appears to wax full and wane to a crescent every month. Cats know this and will be impressed that you've worked it out as well.

ingredients

a ball of dark blue, night sky-coloured wool
a ball of silvery moon-coloured wool
2 cardboard circles, 12.5cm (5in) in diameter with a circle 5cm
(2in) in diameter cut out from the middle
3 single pieces of raffia, each about 1m (1 yard) long, plaited

1. With the two circles together, wind the blue wool around one half of the circle and the silver around the other. While at work, occasionally say, "This wool, symbolic of the moon, binds us to the task. No more will [cat's name] be tempted to go where he's not asked."

2. When you have filled the holes with wool, use sharp scissors to cut through the wool around the edge, between the two layers of card, and say, "The circle is undone, the magic is done, the moon pompom spell it has begun."

3. Between the layers of card, tie the raffia to secure the wool very tightly. Remove the card and say, "Bright blessings to our moon pompom. Let play commence." Your moon pompom is ready and charged for action. Whenever you need to distract, walk around trailing the pompom in a clockwise spiral and await the arrival of cat.

Lucky cat amulet

We tend to think only black cats are lucky. But they're all naturally lucky because they have a positive approach to life. As the old adage goes, "There's none so lucky as a cat that thinks himself lucky."

This Gnostic charm, when attached to a collar, may bring further luck to a cat and to all whose path he crosses.

ingredients
a small piece of handmade paper
red ink

1. On the paper write

ABLANATHANALBA
BLANATHANALB
LANATHANAL
ANATHANA
NATHAN
ATHA
TH

2. Roll up the paper, place in a name-tag cylinder and attach to the cat's collar.

Crossed
legs spell

Just one tomcat in the neighbourhood can cause just one female to mother hundreds of kittens and be great-great-grandmother to thousands of others in her lifetime. There just aren't enough homes. They will die from starvation and disease.

Once neutered, a tom is less likely to be injured in scraps or run over while out on the pull. Spayed females won't have unwanted litters to worry about and can concentrate on careers such as mousing or posing as garden ornaments. Both sexes will be grateful.

Try this spell before going to the vet's, to help the operation go smoothly and aid recuperation.

ingredients
white flower petals & **a white candle**
white thread & **fur from cat**

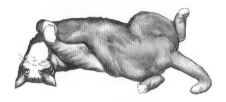

1. Scatter petals in the shape of an ankh cross and tie the fur to the candle with white thread. Place the candle within the circle of the cross and light it, saying, "The ankh gives and protects all life. In this symbol and by the Spirit [cat's name] be blessed. Though you shall come home well with one bit less."

2. When the candle burns down through the hair and thread the spell is cast.

Fleas away

There are plenty of chemicals available to ward off fleas. Natural magic can be just as effective, especially if you act before the warm summer months when the flea breeding season gets under way. The lavender mat will cause fleas to flee as well as giving cats the sweetest scent.

1. Poke the lavender stalks through the hessian until the material is covered with lavender blooms. Turn over and stitch stalks to the cloth.

2. The mat will be more effective and extremely enjoyable if placed near an aga. Open fires are a bit dicey, since the mat is inflammable.

Shooo flies

If a cat fails to polish off his food in one sitting, remove the plate and refrigerate until the next meal time. Never leave cat food – not even dry biscuits – lying about all day. It encourages on-and-off snacking, which is a sure way to find yourself living with an obese cat.

   Discarded food also attracts flies. Yuck. The thing I really can't stand is when people set cat food down near litter trays and then go out for the day. No no no no no.

ingredients
a bunch of tansy

Look out for tansy (*Tanacetum vulgare*), with its frothy
dark green foliage and yellow flowers, in herb sections of
garden centres. Tie it in a big bunch and hang near feeding
areas or litter trays. It's totally unfussy about growing
conditions.

This is an ancient spell to keep the flies at bay.

Old cat retirement patch

Help a cat make the most of his twilight years with this herbal bed guaranteed to attract butterflies, soothe rheumatic aches and inspire the sweetest dreams. Locate it in a sunny, sheltered corner of the garden.

ingredients
a mound of earth
thyme seeds or cuttings
dwarf lavender

1. If using thyme seeds, plant them indoors or under glass. Harden off before planting out on the earth mound. Plant the lavender around the mound.

2. The thyme will grow and spread to form a carpet, which will release soothing oils as the cat sleeps on it.

3. Dead-head the flowers as they fade to ensure that the thyme carpet remains thick the following year.

An elderly cat may be too creaky to lurch at butterflies, but just watching can be entertainment enough.

An udjat eye for protection

Udjat in Egyptian means "making better". According to legend, Horus, the falcon God, lost his eye. Fortunately the Goddess Hathor restored his sight. The eye symbol has since been used as a symbol of healing and protection for at least 8000 years, often appearing on jewellery.

An udjat also used to be wrapped up with mummies to protect the "dead" in the next life.

ingredients

**any medium with which to create the symbol
(it could be made from clay and painted with enamels, cast from silver or drawn on card and coloured in with crayons. It's not too difficult to buy an udjat, either)**

1. Either attach to a collar, pin to a sick bed or, if a cat is off his food, paint it on a feeding bowl.

2. If a stray cat is coming into your home uninvited, paint an udjat eye at cat height on outside doors and cat flaps.

Cat flu spell

Although vaccines are available for both the mild and the serious strains of cat flu, they are expensive and don't provide life-long immunity. Which is why not all cats are vaccinated.

Kittens are especially vulnerable if they live with older vaccinated cats who can carry the virus home on their coats. Even humans in contact with a carrier can pass it on to cats via clothing.

With prompt veterinary attention and careful nursing, most cats will recover, although they may have runny noses and eyes for the rest of their lives.

This Gnostic spell, from the 2nd century AD, is said to ward off illness and cure a fever in nine days.

ingredients
paper & **red ink** & **ribbon**

1. Copy the following on to the paper:

ABRACADABRA
BRACADABRA
RACADABRA
ACADABRA
CADABRA
ADABRA
DABRA
ABRA
BRA
RA
A

2. Using the ribbon, attach the paper to the cat's collar.

3. After nine days take the paper to an eastward flowing stream and toss it over your shoulder. The heat of the fever is returned to the source of all warmth: the sun.

Pill popper

However lethargic a sick cat, when the medicine arrives they're all able to race round the walls and hang from an overhead light-fitting until you swear you've flushed the tablets down the toilet.

Stealth is the key word. Have everything to hand before the cat senses your guilt and heads for the chandelier.

ingredients

a polo-necked jumper & **lavender oil**
white candle & **tablet**
possibly gloves if the cat is a biter

1. Heat the oil on a burner. Light the candle, saying, "I wish this cat well with this spell. No harm shall be done. With one small swallow good will overcome."

2. Pull the jumper over the cat's head and wrap the arms around him. Place the cat face down on the floor and kneel over him. So long as he can't wriggle out of the jumper, there is no escape. Lift his head so his nose points to the ceiling.

3. Poke a finger into the side of his mouth and prise open with the ancient words: "Open sesame." Slip in a pill, keep his head pointing skywards and stroke his throat until he visibly gulps. Repeat as necessary.

Tom's poultice

To the uninitiated a witch's bubbling cauldron might be cooking anything from newts' eyes to frogs' tongues. Brews were more likely, however, to be secret herbal healing remedies.

Because tomcats love to scrap, they're forever developing abscesses on their faces, which often still contain the claw of their foe. This poultice, which relies on the natural magical properties of herbs, is perfect for drawing out the wound. I developed it for Tom, a gorgeous cat who could never keep out of trouble, providing me with hours of pleasure tending his boils.

ingredients
a handful of chamomile flowers
**a handful of bruised thyme (pick the heads, not whole
sprigs, since this allows the thyme to grow better)**
muslin bag

Place the herbs in the bag and steep in boiling water for
a few minutes. Gently remove excess water, allow poultice
to cool and apply to the abscess. Do not squeeze, but mop
up the pus as it oozes out.

Calendula cream may be daubed on the wound.

Hot cat summer soother

Keep a cat cool with this special herbal treat which is just as effective on humans – add a few cubes to a long cold drink.

ingredients
a packet of organic mother-of-thyme seeds

42

1. Sew and nurture the thyme
   in top-quality organic soil
   (peat-free, of course), feed with
   good-quality organic fertiliser
   (bat guano is good). Plant out
   when the seedlings are strong enough.

2. When plants come into flower, pick them immediately
   and freeze in ice cubes.

3. On a hot summer's day, pop a few in the cat's water bowl.
   Rosemary and catnip flowers are just as good. Yes, you
   can cheat and buy plants instead of seeds, but it won't be
   so magical, because you and the cat won't have been
   involved in the growing process.

Traffic talisman

Roads present cats with the greatest modern danger. While many cats do develop a modicum of road sense, at night they can be dazzled by headlights, which roots them to the spot. I won't go on.

If you offer food at the same time each evening, cats get so prompt you'd think they had a wristwatch stashed under their collar. This is a good way to encourage them to spend dark evenings indoors. Generally, however, deterring cats from roaming in the direction of roads is your best bet.

ingredients
water-filled clear glass bottles with stoppers
(placed in any border these will also stop cats fouling)
chive plants & a bunch of sage

Plant chives along the boundary between your home and the road, and place the bottles in between. In the windows of the road-side of your home, hang a bunch of sage to bring luck to all inhabitants who are out and about.

Curiosity . . .

I spent many childhood hours mourning the cats who surely died in the search for birthday presents under my parents' bed. My heart also went out to the cats who shuffled off this mortal coil, with one last thought, "I wonder what happens if I press this?"

I realise my mother grossly exaggerated the effects of curiosity. But it can cause problems, like being locked in potting sheds or getting stuck to newly fixed pottery with a face-full of superglue.

ingredients
5 spiral seashells & **5 small bells**
driftwood & **white thread**

1. Make a mobile with the ingredients. As you work, say,
   "'Tis never the curiosity that sends cats through the vale.
   It's the luck they carry with them as they rest or they
   travail. But t'was never a cat so lucky as the cat who
   thought him so. Thus I call on luck to greet your
   thoughts whenever the wind doth blow."

2. Hang the mobile where the cat and the wind can reach it.

Nine lives top-up

Cats enjoy narrow escapes. Cavalier activities such as getting locked in, dashing in front of moving vehicles and falling from unfeasible heights (off buildings or down wells) give them a real buzz, fuelling their sense of invincibility.

Once a life has been forfeited in such a manner, try this spell to steady your nerves and replenish the cat's luck.

ingredients

8 white candles
a piece of gold thread tied around one red candle
a piece of blue paper decorated with an ankh cross
(illustrated above) and the cat's name
a flameproof bowl to catch the ashes

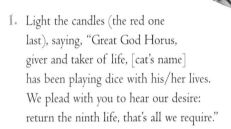

1. Light the candles (the red one
   last), saying, "Great God Horus,
   giver and taker of life, [cat's name]
   has been playing dice with his/her lives.
   We plead with you to hear our desire:
   return the ninth life, that's all we require."

2. Light the paper using the flame from the red candle,
   saying, "When all nine lives are finally spent,
   [cat's name] will come to serve you well. Until that
   time please relent."

3. When the flame burns through the thread, the cat has
   nine lives once more. Suggest that he be more careful in
   future. But don't expect him to listen.

Wild bird spell

Witches believe that if you wish someone harm, something three times as bad may happen to you. If you ignore an opportunity to do good, you may also be susceptible to karmic retribution.

Cats will hunt. So help the wild birds by supplying a better breeding habitat and food for them. Increased populations means the odd tit or sparrow dropped at your feet as a gift will not cause an irreversible decline in numbers.

ingredients
trees and hedging, some of which should have berries
bird boxes (optional)
a bird table & seeds and food scraps

1. Plant the trees and shrubs and secure boxes to walls or trees. The bird table should be too sturdy for animals or children to knock down and be placed well away from shrubbery where cats can lie in wait.

2. As you put out seeds and fat say, "I call on you, Cernussos, with your energy of creation, talk to the wild birds and bring them salvation. Tell them to fly when the cat is near. Grant them safe passage out of here."

3. In dry summers, place a bowl of water on the bird table.

Diana's hunting spell

We're horrified when cats get their claws into wild birds. But we should rejoice when mice, rats and rabbits (not pet ones) are brought home. So long as they're dead.

I once lived with a cat who favoured seagulls, a difficult prey to drag through cat flaps. What a pity cats won't admit to knowing the difference between a pest and an endangered species – or a nice snake and a nasty one. This spell might help.

ingredients
a full moon
3 blood red candles

1. Working by moonlight, light the candles, saying, "Diana of the moon, great mother of the gods, life is taken and given by your light. As we adore you as divine, let [cat's name]'s hunting be sublime. Hide the snakes in the dark of night. Let live the frogs and birds. 'Tis right. But by your light so pure and bright guide [cat's name] to the rats and mice."

2. Let the candles burn down to their ends.

Impossibly forgiving

A neighbour's prized ornamental goldfish, a child's budgerigar, a rare South American flycatcher blown off course and being observed by birders: just some of the prey taken down by feline instinct. Oh the horror.

Then there's the Thanksgiving turkey, the mother-in-law's birthday cake and the one that didn't get away, proudly brought home from a fishing trip. Great game for a cat. A nightmare for human friends.

ingredients

pink flowers & **a black candle**
a mirror & **rainwater or dew**

1. Outdoors, put the mirror on the ground. Place the candle in the centre of the mirror, scatter the flowers around it and sprinkle with water.

2. Sit peacefully. Breathe deeply. Say, "You cannot tame Spirit. You cannot blame Spirit. Though this act is my bane I proclaim to the skies, this anger I feel is but love in disguise. Isis, Osiris please forgive me as I must forgive [cat's name]. Blessed be."

To banish foul bane

The doing and burying of a cat's ordure was once carried out with the utmost discretion. Of late, however, cats appear happy to "go" anywhere, leaving their manure exposed where children and grown-ups can walk in it or worse, should we dare to garden with our gloves off.

Perhaps the introduction of cat-litter trays, often stored in kitchens of all places, has left cats confused about what is and what is not hygienically acceptable.

If you're a victim of bad cat toilet habits, try this spell which has a yuck factor of its own but is highly effective.

❖

ingredients

a pint of "processed" chamomile tea

1. Clear away all cat mess. If patios and paths are affected, hose down and disinfect. Drink the herb tea. When you need to go, catch the pee in a pot.

2. Pour this effective repellent on to soil around your boundaries, saying, "Away cats. If you know what's good, show respect for this neighbourhood. Any feline who ignores this threat shall be punished by the great Bastet."

Righteous habit, wrong place

Cats need to scratch. It builds healthy claws, so essential to their balance and for defending themselves when necessary.

Clawing furniture is exasperating. But if your feline friend does indulge, please do not retaliate by declawing his front paws – a practice all too common in the United States, but banned in the UK. A cat minus his claws is a cat unable to jump, spring and race around without fear of falling over. His life purpose is drained. Depression, loss of interest in food and antisocial behaviour will inevitably follow such a cruel procedure.

Instead, take a deep breath and enjoy the process of choosing new upholstery. Meanwhile, treat your cat to the user-friendly natural magic in this spell.

ingredients

an apple log, about 60cm (2ft) long
a hemp-plaited rope about 1m (3-4ft) long
13 sprigs of catmint & brown paper & 4 large brown stones

1. Lay out the brown paper and secure at each corner with the stones. Strew the catmint over the paper, then roll the rope over the catmint, saying, "May the God and Goddess known to the cat bless this rope and bring us hope. Protect my home by your magical lores, make this a sanctuary for cat's claws."

2. Wrap the rope and catmint in the paper overnight. The following day, tie the rope to one end of the apple log. Wind it along its length, saying, "This rope binds the spell. Should all go well, 'tis here the cat shall scratch and claw and never again will chairs be used, nor tables, cloth nor door."

3. Repeat the chant until the rope is wound around the log and secured with a flourish of a knot.

Cats should need little encouragement to scratch away. However, some may still refuse to give up on the furniture. Protect your property with a firm call of "no" and a clap of your hands when the talons come out elsewhere. By the same token, when the cat utilises the apple log, purr your contentment.

High-rise spell

It borders on cruelty to bring an adult cat with previous outdoor experience indoors full time. A kitten born in a skyscraper may be better suited to the lifestyle. But it's still far from ideal.

This herbal healing box will make life easier to cope with for high-rise cats.

ingredients

earth-filled window-box
chives, fennel, tarragon, catmint and thyme
5 spiral seashells & 3 crystals

1. The herbs may be varied, but fennel and tarragon are firm favourites with cats since they go so well with fish.

2. After planting up the box, lay the shells and crystals on the soil, saying, "May the elements be present in this home, creating balance for the cat who cannot roam. May the sea and the rocks and flora be known, especially when [cat's name] is here alone."

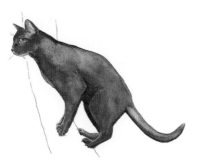

Remember that plants need plenty of natural light, regular watering and organic feed. Keep turning the box round so that the plants don't just grow in one direction.

Travel cat

My childhood cat mates thoroughly enjoyed a change of scenery whether we were boating down a river or building sandcastles at the seaside. Much better than getting a neighbour round to feed them or booking them into a cattery.

Cats must travel in baskets, lined with plenty of newspaper to soak up accidents. Loose in a car is a tragic idea – they might escape from a window or get under the driver's feet, making braking impossible.

If a cat has only ever been taken to a vet, he may misinterpret your offer of a vacation and disappear off into the undergrowth for a day – very frustrating when you're packed and ready to go. So prepare cats with plenty of short fun trips first.

ingredients

an amethyst crystal

1. Charge the crystal under a full moon, saying, "Goddess charm this crystal by your light. Keep [cat's name] safe both day and night."

2. Place the crystal in the cage when you leave home.

Cerridwen's shape-shifting spell

How can a cat get any sleep when there's a child pulling his tail, or a dog sniffing his private parts all day?

This spell allows a cat to go unnoticed for as long as he cares to be left alone.

ingredients
silver foil & **a tray** & **sand**

1. Cover the tray with foil and sprinkle the sand quite thickly into it.

2. Draw a pentacle in the sand and encourage the cat to walk across it, saying, "By the power of Cerridwen may you too be able to shift your shape like sand. Be disguised from the eyes of those who'd make you ache. And be not touched by groping hands."

Scaredy cat

Timidity in a feline is usually a symptom of trauma. Perhaps the cat was bullied or mistreated as a kitten, had a near-death experience, or was severely ill.

Whatever the cause, it is very frustrating for all concerned when visitors expect a robust greeting but are met by a shivering wreck who may bite and scratch if cornered in the quest for a cuddle.

ingredients

a small amethyst pendant
lavender oil
soothing music, preferably Tibetan

1. Heat the oil in a burner, play the music softly and rub the pendant on the cat, speaking to him in soothing tones. Tibetan music is excellent since the instruments and voices invoke the elements. Very magical.

2. Repeat every day for a month, if you can manage this with no loud or disturbing interruptions. Attach the pendant to the cat's collar in between sessions.

3. When you expect visitors, heat the oil and play the music. Advise everyone to ignore the cat. He may eventually come to them or walk past, tail and head held high, to show that he is overcoming his timidity but is not yet ready to converse.

Lie down dog

Dogs, like cats, are prone to letting their instincts get the better of them. One particular primeval itch that screams to be scratched is the desire to chase anything that streaks across a dog's line of vision: cars, tractors, rabbits, postmen. And cats.

Kittens can easily be killed by dogs. Adult cats, however, can run and jump for it or avoid certain gardens altogether. Easier said than done when a dog and cat share the same territory.

ingredients
a nail
a hair from the dog
white thread

1. Bind the hair on to the nail with the thread, saying, "Good dog, we wish you no ill, but implore you be still. This thread it binds you to our will."

2. Bang the nail into the ground, saying, "Until this nail is found, when [cat's name] is around, you shall lie down."

Cat/dog
love potion

Some cats and dogs get on. Many more need gentle persuasion.
Try this love potion to open their eyes to the beauty of each other.

ingredients
3 sprigs of vervain leaves & **3 hairs from each animal**
the heart of a lamb or calf & **red rose petals**

1. Boil the heart with the vervain leaves and the animal hairs. Stir the brew, saying, "By Cernussos shall your eyes and hearts be open to love. No more the bark, or screech or bite, as teeth do gnash and fur does fly. From now on you shall greet the other with purrs and licks and whines of delight."

2. Divide the heart between the beasts and pour on the liquid, which may be soaked up with biscuit. Sprinkle rose petals around their bowls before serving.

Bully
bane hex

Occasionally a rogue cat will stroll into your home, steal your food and the cat's, beat you all up, spray, pooh and leave. Humans are reduced to tears while cats are rendered nervous wrecks.

Speak to the cat's human house mates and if he's (very likely) a tom discuss having his bits chopped off (by a qualified vet rather than a local vigilante). But with emotions running high you may consider this hex – a dramatic course of action for only the most exasperating of cases.

ingredients
fur from the tomcat
melted wax & **black thread** & **a nail**

1. As the wax cools, add the fur. When it's hard enough to mould, form it into the shape of a cat.

2. Bind the thread around the model, saying, "With this thread I bind you to our will." Repeat seven times.

3. Nail to a territorial tree or fencepost, saying, "By Nut shall you be stilled. You [use name if you know it] foul creature of our bane. You are done if still you come. Come and you'll feel pain."

Stray cat divination

When a cat goes missing, you might simply have been sacked because the catering's better elsewhere.

Go in search, put up posters, knock on doors. Only you can decide how long you are prepared to play the waiting game. But deep inside your heart you probably know what's happened. This ancient Egyptian divination method may help you to realise this.

ingredients
**3 black candles
cat's bowl filled with a bottle of black ink
and topped up with water
a sprig of sage**

1. Hang the sage up in a window. Working with the candles behind you, sit with your cat's magic blanket if he has one. Breathe in through your nose and out through your mouth seven times.

2. Stare into the blackened water and call out to your cat, saying, "In the darkness I call to your light. Shine your light on me now that I may see."

3. Try not to block the images that come to you. It is better to know. Now you must act upon your intuitive discovery.

Funeral reading

This reading is from a song engraved upon the wall of a pharaoh's tomb around 4000 years ago. It may be read at the burial of a body, the scattering of ashes, or when a cat has been missing for so long you decide it's time for a goodbye ritual.

It tells us not to grieve, but to make the most of our lives before we follow the cat.

Close your eyes and recall your fondest memories.
Scatter ashes or bury a memento or the remains.

Say, "No one cometh back from below, no one who might
say what it is like, who might tell us what they need to calm
our hearts until the time when we shall go also there wither
they have gone.

"So, be gay and follow thy desires while thou livest, pour
myrrh upon thy hair. Do what thou wilt upon earth and wear
not out thine heart until the day of lamentation be come.
In the land of silence, the god of implacable heart, Osiris of
the Dead, hears no lamentation. Plaints can save no one.
Behold! Make happy thy day. Be not eaten up with care."

You may like to add "Amen" to this, since it finishes it off
in a way we expect.

Herb garden memorial

Those made of stern stuff will plant this herb garden upon a cat's grave, which will be rich in nutrients. Alternatively choose a sunny border.

ingredients
**large flat white stones, about 5cm/2in in diameter
1 rosemary plant, 5 thyme plants, 3 sage plants
and 2 catnip plants**

1. Trace a pentacle in the soil and outline with the stones. Plant the rosemary in the middle, the thyme at each of the five points and the sage and catmint alternately between the thyme plants.

2. When finished, water generously, saying, "After life comes death and after death comes life. As [cat's name] has passed on through the vale, so shall we all when time prevails.

"With rosemary I remember, with sage I am soothed, the mint is for friendship and thyme to heal."

Attracting the right cat mate

Cats prefer to choose their human companions. But you are entitled to an opinion since gender, breeding and age (of both cat and human) will influence the relationship considerably.

ingredients
**a dark blue candle
paper and blue ink
a flame-proof bowl to catch ashes**

1. Prior to visiting potential cat mates, in a darkened room light the candle and meditate on the following:

   Females are homely, while males prefer to wander and fight, incurring endless vet bills even when neutered.

   Persian and British or American short-hair types tend to be loyal lap-lovers, while oriental short-hairs prefer head-sitting and can be more exasperating than human toddlers.

   If you keep dogs, kittens should be avoided since they may resemble toys, or lunch!

2. Write five key words on the paper describing your perfect cat mate, then hold it over the bowl and set fire to it, saying, "Bastet, bless us all and allow us all to recognise the call when the right cat arrives to rule."

Space cleansing

An apparent stray turns up in the garden, you feed him a couple of times and the next thing you know you're fighting for the pillow in your own bed.

When a new cat or kitten arrives, whether invited or not, it's good to cleanse the space to get things off to an harmonious start. This is also an excellent spell for a new litter (waft the smoke prior to their birth, though).

ingredients

a sage stick

1. Sage sticks can be bought from occult shops. To make your own, dry seven long stems of sage in a warm dark place for about five days before binding together with thread.

2. Light the sage stick (you want it smoking, not in flames) and waft it through the home, saying, "This sacred sage revered by humans and known to cats, will cleanse this home of negative energies and allow our spirits to fly with ease. May [cat's name] enjoy this new domain, living a long happy life, all free from bane."

Sage often has the effect of inspiring you to spring clean. Go with it.

Naming

ceremony

Most human cultures have rituals for naming children, often combined with an initiation into a particular religion.

We can't do this with cats since they know more than we do about the true mysteries of creation and have their own magical religion far too complex for us humans to comprehend.

We can, however, give cats a name and ask the Spirit, in all its guises, to protect the animal.

ingredients

**a cat with no name
butter**

1. Take the cat on your lap and stroke him, saying, "Cat, we ask the Spirit to watch over you and guide you through a long, contented life. May you make good decisions like leave the birds but catch the mice. May your health never fail until your time comes to pass on through the vale. In the name of the God and Goddess we name you [new name]. Blessed be [cat's name]. You are truly blessed."

2. Anoint the cat by rubbing butter on his nose (said to keep a cat close to home).

New cat on the block

If you already have cat mates, introduce a newcomer without fanfare and fuss to minimise jealousy. Cats should soon put aside differences to celebrate their similarities.

In the neighbourhood, you can't be paw-holding. There's nothing worse than being seen with an over-anxious human – remember how you felt when Mum insisted on walking you to the school gates. Instead, cast this protective spell.

ingredients

sea salt & **5 purple candles** & **a crystal**

1. Sprinkle the salt in the shape of a pentacle on a floor,
   place the crystal in the centre and the candles on each
   point of the star.

2. Lure the cat into the centre with a tidbit. Imagine a
   golden light rising up around the circle. Tell the cat,
   "Protected by the Spirit's energies, you are safe from
   your enemies. Should danger come,
   the Spirit will raise the alarm.
   For blessed by the Goddess
   Bastet you are and so shall
   be kept from harm."

   When he goes out for a
   stroll, envisage this golden
   light encircling the cat.

Six sabbats for cats

Sabbats are high days, holidays and feast days to celebrate the turning of the wheel of the year. As the seasons change, so do the tasks, and rewards.

Through ritual and symbolism, sabbats have for thousands of years taught us the true meaning of what life is all about: surviving and making the most of it.

Because the sabbat tradition developed in the northern hemisphere, the direct associations with the farming calender fail to apply in places like Australia. So many pagan antipodeans swap them all around. Yule becomes Midsummer since 21 December is the longest day in Australia and New Zealand. Lughnasa is celebrated on 1 February, Samhain 30 May, Imbolg 1 August and Beltane 31 October.

Samhain, 31 October

Cats remember loved ones who have passed on through the vale.
It's a great time for hunting in cold climates, since mice and
other fauna come in from the fields to winter indoors.

On what we now call Halloween, strew the cat's bed with
chrysanthemums. Light three orange candles and a fire (a
radiator will do if there's somewhere to snuggle beside it).
Lay out the magic blanket, feed the cat pâté and catnip and
allow him to commune with his ancestors.

Winter solstice, 21 December

The shortest day of the year. The longest night.

Decorate a tree indoors with strings of popcorn and toy
mice. Kittens in particular love the acrobatic possibilities of
aiming for the star at the top. Light black candles to symbolise
the rebirth of light as we head towards summer.

Imbolg, 31 January

The earth tingles with renewed life and is
set to blossom into spring. This day is also dedicated to the
moon goddess in all her guises, as well as women in general.

A cat may wear a white ribbon and white flowers in place of
a collar. Fill your home with white candles. Plant some catnip
seeds indoors on a window-sill so that you and the cat may
witness the coming of spring.

Beltane, 1 May

Balmy nights, sun-soaked afternoons, bright mornings.
They're all on their way. Sew bells on various coloured
ribbons and attach to a stick. As the cat plays he will be
performing his own brand of Morris come maypole
dancing – both traditions of this day.

Pâté and catnip may once again be eaten.

Harden off your catnip seedlings and plant
outdoors if you have a garden.

Summer solstice, 21 June

At dawn go outside with the cat and call out to Ra, the
Egyptian sun god. Place a mirror where it may capture the sun's
rays all day. In the winter you can bring out the mirror for the
cat to gaze into to derive spiritual warmth.

At sunset, return to the garden with the cat. Make a flail with a
bunch of catnip and raffia. Thwack the cat with it, saying,
"Ra, ra ra ra ra ra ra." The neighbours will think
you're bonkers, but cats will love you.

Lughnasa, 1 August

Strictly speaking, this is a two-week festival beginning
around 15 July when lavender is traditionally gathered.

So on 1 August or before, light some coals in the garden and
grill fish flavoured with fennel and tarragon for the local cats.

Play your cat mate's favourite tunes (what do you mean you
don't know? Find out) and dance the reeling midnight through.

You could jump over a bonfire together, to ward off
fleas and other parasites. But only if the cat is of a strong
emotional disposition.

Glossary

Ankh an ancient symbol predating, but much used by, the Ancient
Egyptians. Sometimes referred to as a cross, representing life,
man and woman as well as cosmic knowledge. It's a sort of key
to unlock the secret mysteries of the universe. Now we just
have to find the lock.

Bastet Egyptian cat goddess. Cats were considered her
representatives on earth. Consequently they were treated with
the respect they deserve in life and mummified at death

Catnip aka catmint, catnep or *Nepeta cataria*. A hardy perennial
herbaceous herb with aromatic, downy leaves and blue or white
flowers. Cats love it.

Cerwidwen Welsh Celtic goddess, the wise old woman, associated
with shape-shifting and the cauldron of knowledge: in other
words metamorphosis, physical, mental and spiritual.

Cernussos ancient horned god of wild animals, hunting and
fertility and consort to the Mother Goddess. Worshipped
throughout Britain and Celtic Europe, cats have long considered
him a cat-friendly deity, especially thanking him for all the mice.

Diana Roman moon goddess, a huntress and protector of animals. Also known as a helper of underdogs, guarding peasants from cruel feudal lords, for example.

Elements earth, air, fire and water. All four are needed to sustain life. Each must be balanced but that doesn't necessarily mean equal parts of each. The elements are used symbolically in spells to represent the natural world and the Spirit.

Freya northern European goddess of love and magic who rode a chariot drawn by cats.

Hathor Egyptian mother goddess of all pharaohs, cow goddess and wife of Horus.

Horus falcon god, an Egyptian deity, the son of Isis and Osiris, and ruler of the skies above. He lost an eye and was healed by his wife Hathor.

Isis Egyptian archetypal mother/fertility/nature goddess, and mother of the falcon god, Horus. He was often depicted seated upon his mother's knee and together they are believed to be the prototype for the modern-day icon of madonna and child.

Nut mother of Isis and the mother of all mother goddesses. Symbolised by a cow jumping over a moon.

Osiris Egyptian archetypal father/fertility/nature god, consort to

Isis and father of Horus. He died and was brought back to life by Isis. He symbolises life after death, or rebirth.

Pentacle five-pointed star within a circle representing the magical energies of the universe. Each point represents one of the four elements, plus Spirit. Traditionally used in Celtic and Wiccan magic, but similar star iconography is found in most religious cultures.

Spiral an ancient symbol representing life, its continuation and renewal. Moving in a spiral allows one to build up magical energies and a sense of belonging. Dancing in spirals is an almost universal practice among modern and primitive cultures alike.

Spirit the fifth element or essence. It represents the space in which all things are contained and the energy responsible for creation.

Thoth Egyptian moon god of words, magic and scribes. In the underworld he records the names of souls.

Udjat the eye of Horus worn or painted upon surfaces to ward off danger and welcome good health and great fortune. The Egyptians sent their dead off with an udjat in their sarcophagus to guard them in the next life.

Vale, the as in "pass through the vale". An archaic phrase encompassing all beliefs, and meaning to die, to leave this world and pass on to the next, wherever and whatever that may be.

Getting in Touch

Any questions regarding magic and cats? You can contact Daisy Pepper via email: **daisypepper@emara.com**